Fat

Quick And Easy Low-Carb High-Fat Sweet And Savory Ketogenic Fat Bombs

Steve Lawson

TERMS & CONDITIONS

Table Of Contents

Chapter 1 – Fat Bombs

Thanks for purchasing my book. Now go ahead and check these fantastic fat bomb recipes.

Astonishing The Keto Banana Loaf

Legend overload…

Ingredients:

- 5 large eggs
- A cup of whole almond meal.
- A cup of mashed 3 large bananas
- A cup of unprocessed wheat bran, and
- 1/2 cup of soy protein powder
- About 1.5 teaspoon of baking powder
- 2 teaspoons of grated lemon peel
- A teaspoon of baking powder
- About 4.5 teaspoons of Splenda (sugar substitute)
- 12 ounces of soft cream cheese

Directions:

1. First of all, please make sure you have all the ingredients available. Pre-heat the oven to about 310 to 320 degree F, & then butter lightly, the mini loaf pans.
2. Then cut some strips of waxed paper to fit the bottoms of the pan, & allow them to hang over the edges.
3. This step is important. Get the cream cheese & eggs in the electric mixer bowl, and beat until flat.
4. Now add the remaining eggs (one at a time), add all other ingredients & then beat at a slow speed.
5. One thing remains to be done now. Add the nuts & bran and spoon the batter into the pans.
6. Finally bake the bread for about an hour until done & serve immediately.

Preparation time: 1 hour

Servings: 3 to 4

Most fantastic recipe ever.

Excellent Blackberry Fat Bombs

Nostalgic feeling…

Ingredients:

- 1/2 cup blackberries, fresh or frozen
- About 1 teaspoon of vanilla extract
- 1 cup coconut oil
- About 1.5 tablespoon lemon juice
- 1/2 teaspoon of stevia
- 1 cup coconut butter

Directions:

1. First of all, please make sure you have all the ingredients available. Use a saucepan to melt coconut oil & coconut butter with blackberries over medium heat.
2. Then you should make sure that they are well combined.
3. Transfer the mixture to a blender.
4. This step is important. Add all the other ingredients & puree until smooth.

5. Now use parchment paper to line a baking sheet.
6. Spread the mixture over it & place it in the freezer for about 60 to 90 minutes.
7. Then you want the mixture to solidify before taking it out of the fridge.
8. One thing remains to be done now. Cut it into squares before serving.
9. Finally make sure not to keep it out of the fridge for long.

Serves: 14 to 16

Jumpstart your taste. ?

Legendary Keto Mediterranean Fat Bomb

Simplicity is best.

Ingredients:

- Salt to taste
- About 1/2 cup butter at room temperature (use ghee alternatively)
- 4 pitted olives
- Freshly ground black pepper
- About 3.5 tablespoons chopped herbs (basil, oregano and/or thyme)
- 5 tablespoons grated parmesan cheese
- 4 pieces of drained sun-dried tomatoes
- 2 crushed garlic cloves
- 1/2 cup full-fat cream cheese

Directions:

1. First of all, please make sure you have all the ingredients available. Now quickly use a knife to cut the

butter into small pieces & mix it in a bowl with cream cheese.

2. Now if it is thick, you can leave it on the counter for about half an hour to soften.

3. Once it softened enough, use a fork to mash it & make sure it is well combined.

4. This step is important. Add olives and tomatoes. Next, add the herbs & garlic and season it to taste with pepper and salt.

5. Then combine the ingredients well.

6. Place it into the refrigerator to cool down for about half an hour.

7. Now once the mixture is solid, take it out of the fridge & start making balls.

8. You can use a scooper or a spoon.

9. There should be enough of the mixture to make 5 balls.

10. One thing remains to be done now. Roll each ball in Parmesan cheese & set it on a plate.
11. Finally you can serve immediately or keep in the fridge for up to 7 days.

Serves: 5 to 7

Oh yeah. This is the recipe I was waiting for.

Awesome Tasty Almond Joy Fat Bomb

Legendary taste.

Ingredients:

Topping:

- 1 2/3 c coconut flakes, unsweetened
- About 1.5 tsp vanilla
- 7 tbsp coconut oil
- 1/3 c sweetener
- 2 tsp arrowroot powder

Base:

- 1/2 c coconut oil
- 3 tbsp extra sweetener
- 6 tbsp cocoa
- 1/2 c almond butter
- 1/4 c granulated sweetener
- About 1.5 tsp vanilla

Directions:

For the base:

1. First of all, please make sure you have all the ingredients available. Melt the nut butter & oil together in a pot.
2. Now mix in the cocoa & the granulated sweetener until thoroughly mixed.
3. Stir in all the other base ingredients, except for the vanilla.
4. This step is important. Stir it continuously until it starts to thicken slightly.
5. Then take off the heat & mix in the vanilla.
6. Pour the chocolate into an 8 by 8 baking dish & slide into the freezer to harden as you make the topping.
7. One thing remains to be done now. If you can't fit it in your freezer, you can place in the refrigerator.
8. Finally it will still harden enough to work with.

For the topping:

1. First of all, please make sure you have all the ingredients available. Place the oil in a small skillet & melt.
2. Then mix in the coconut flakes. Add in all the rest of the topping ingredients.
3. Simmer and allow the mixture to thicken a little.
4. This step is important. Make sure you stir constantly. After the base layer has hardened, gently place the coconut mixture over the top.
5. Now if you want to, you can place slivered almonds on top.
6. Place the bars back into the freezer or the refrigerator until they have hardened.
7. One thing remains to be done now. Slice the bars into squares.
8. Finally keep them stored in the refrigerator.

Light taste.

Quick Mouth-Watering Orange Butter Pecans

As the name suggests….

Ingredients:

- 4 pecan halves
- About 1 tsp orange zest
- 1/2 tbsp. unsalted butter
- 1 oz Neufchatel cheese
- Sea salt

Directions:

1. First of all, please make sure you have all the ingredients available. Toast pecans in an oven heated to about 340 to 350 for about 10 to 15 minutes.
2. Now allow to cool.
3. This step is important. Soften cream cheese & butter.
4. One thing remains to be done now. Then add orange zest & mix well until creamy.

5. Finally spread the mixture on a pecan half & top with a sprinkle of sea salt & top with another half.

Servings: 2 to 4

Magical…

Wonderful Butter Pecan White Chocolate Fat Bombs

Right on track.

Ingredients:

- 1/2 cup pecans (Chopped)
- 1/8 teaspoon salt
- About 2.5 tablespoons butter
- 2 tablespoons coconut oil
- 1/8 teaspoon liquid artificial sweetener of choice
- About 2.5 tablespoons powdered sugar substitute of your choice
- 2 ounces cocoa butter
- 1/4 teaspoon vanilla extract

Directions:

1. First of all, please make sure you have all the ingredients available. Add the butter, cocoa butter, & coconut oil to a small pan and warm them over medium heat until they have all melted.

2. Now turn off the stove & add the powdered sweetener to the melted butters. Then, stir in the salt.
3. Next, stir in the liquid sweetener & the vanilla extract.
4. This step is important. Once all the ingredients are well-combined, set the mixture to the side for a moment.
5. Then distribute the chopped pecans among candy molds or silicone mini cupcake molds.
6. Pour in the white chocolate mixture & transfer to the freezer immediately.
7. One thing remains to be done now. Freeze for about 30 to 35 minutes before enjoying & store in the freezer.
8. Finally these will melt very easily, though this makes for a pleasant eating experience.

Believe me…

Elegant Super-Easy Creamy Fudge

Always kept wondering how it was made… One day I sat beside my chef and got it.

Ingredients:

- 6 tbsp unsalted butter
- 2 tsp vanilla extract
- About 1.5 tbsp corn starch
- 1 1/2 erythritol
- 2/3 cup natural peanut butter
- 6 tbsp cream cheese
- About 1.5 pinch of salt

Directions:

1. First of all, please make sure you have all the ingredients available. Put the butter & cream cheese in a pan and heat over medium heat till they are completely melted.
2. Then add the vanilla extract along with peanut butter & stir well to blend thoroughly.

3. This step is important. Sift the corn starch & powdered sweetener & slowly blend them with the butter mixture.
4. Now it will be best to use a hand blender at this stage of mixing as the device will make the process easy.
5. Line a baking tray with parchment paper & then spread the mixture on it evenly.
6. One thing remains to be done now. Keep it in fridge for at least 5.5 hours so that the mixture solidifies.
7. Finally cut into serving size & enjoy!

Total time: 15 to 20 mins

Servings: 2 to 4

Stylish.

Nutrition per Serving:

Protein: 1.6g

Fat: 29g

Carbohydrate: 2g Net

Rich Delicious Vanilla Fat Bomb

I bet you'll find it amazing…

Ingredients:

- 10 to 15 drops liquid stevia
- 1 c macadamia nuts, unsalted
- 1 vanilla bean
- 1/4 c extra virgin coconut oil
- 1/4 c butter
- About 2.5 tbsp powdered swerve

Directions:

1. First of all, please make sure you have all the ingredients available. Next, please pulse the macadamia nuts in a food processor or blender until they are smooth.
2. Now place the macadamia nuts in a bowl & mix in the coconut oil and softened butter.
3. This step is important. Mix in the stevia, vanilla bean, & the powdered swerve.

4. Then pour the mixture into mini muffin forms.
5. One thing remains to be done now. Each should hold about a tablespoon & a half.
6. Finally refrigerate for around 30 to 35 minutes & remove from the mold. Keep refrigerated.

Servings: 12 to 14

The hit list recipe.

Titanic Coconut Strawberry Fat Bomb

Some things never fail you.

Ingredients:

- 1 cup coconut butter
- 1/4 tsp. vanilla powder
- About 1 tsp. Sweet Leaf Stevia drops
- 1 tbsp. lime juice
- About 1 cup frozen strawberries
- 1 cup coconut oil

Directions:

1. First of all, please make sure you have all the ingredients available. Take a medium-sized pot & combine coconut oil, coconut butter, and frozen strawberries
2. Now place the pot on heat over medium heat settings until the mixture is combined nicely

3. Put the above-prepared mixture in a small sized blender or in a food processor

4. This step is important. Add lime juice & Stevia drops to the blender

5. Then process the mixture in the food processor until the mixture is soft & smooth

6. Place a parchment paper on a small sized pan

7. Now extract the mixture from the blender & spread it out on the pan over the paper

8. One thing remains to be done now. Put the pan in a refrigerator for about 1 hour until the mixture has hardened

9. Finally take out the hardened mixture from the pan & cut into small, equal sizes and serve

Total cooking & preparation time: 10 to 20 minutes

Total servings: 16 to 18

Mushroom fries bring back a lot of memories.

Nutrition facts (estimated amount per serving)

14.5g Total Fat

12.4g Saturated Fat

1mg Potassium

0g Trans Fat

0.3g Protein

132 Calories

0mg Cholesterol

6g Dietary Fiber

5mg Sodium

3.3g Carbohydrates

1g Sugars

Tasty Amazing Allspice Dark Almond Desire Fat Bombs

My sister makes it every now & then.

Ingredients:

- 1 Tablespoon heavy cream
- 4 to 5 drops liquid sweetener
- About 1.5 Tablespoon coconut oil
- 1/4 teaspoon allspice
- About 1.5 teaspoon cocoa powder
- 2 Tablespoons almond butter

Directions:

1. First of all, please make sure you have all the ingredients available. Next, please put the almond butter into a cup, mold or even a container of your choice

2. Now add the coconut oil, cocoa powder, heavy cream, & allspice to the mixture.
3. This step is important. Mix well
4. One thing remains to be done now. Then freeze for about 2.5 hrs.
5. Finally remove & enjoy

For a eternal experience.

Yummy Delight Coconut And Cinnamon Muffin

Like never before…

Ingredients:

- 2 tablespoons coconut flour
- About 1 teaspoon salt
- 1/2 teaspoon baking powder
- 1 tablespoon shredded coconut, organic
- 1/4 teaspoon cinnamon
- 1/2 cup Swerve / erythritol
- About 1 teaspoon almond extract
- 2 large eggs
- 4 tablespoons coconut oil
- 1 cup almond flour
- 1/2 teaspoon vanilla extract

Directions:

1. First of all, please make sure you have all the ingredients available. Then preheat oven at 340 to 350 degrees.

2. In a bowl add all ingredients & mix well until even.
3. One thing remains to be done now. Now transfer into baking dish & bake for about 15 to 20 minutes.
4. Finally cut into bars Serve & enjoy.

Prep Time: 5 to 10 Minutes

Cooking Time: 15 to 20 Minutes

Serves: 12 to 14

Worth it…

Nutritional Information

Protein: 8 g;

Total Fat: 9.7 g;

Calories 103

Carbohydrates: 0 g;

Unique Blueberry Almond Smoothie

Simple recipe for you…

Ingredients:

- 1 packet artificial sweetener
- 1/2 scoop vanilla whey protein
- 2 oz heavy whipping cream
- About 1.5 cup unsweetened almond milk
- 1/4 cup frozen unsweetened blueberries

Directions:

1. First of all, please make sure you have all the ingredients available. Then put all ingredients in blender & blend until smooth.
2. One thing remains to be done now. Now add a little water if it becomes too thick.
3. Finally enjoy!

Servings: 1 to 3

Cooking Times: 5 to 10 minutes

Delightful…

Nutrition Facts (per serving)

Total Carbohydrates: 14g

Dietary Fiber: 1g

Net Carbs:1,5g

Protein: 7,68

Total Fat: 26g

Calories: 337

Protein 9,38g 19%

.

Ultimate The Ketogenic Oopsie Bread Rolls

For those who're ultra fantastic

Ingredients:

- About 1/4 teaspoon of salt.
- Non-sticky cooking spray,
- 2 1/2 ounces of full-fat cold cubed cream cheese,
- About 1/2 teaspoon of tartar cream,
- 3 medium to large eggs,

Directions:

1. First of all, please make sure you have all the ingredients available. Pre-heat the oven to about 290 to 300 degree F, then line some cookie sheet with parchment paper, before spraying with cooking spray.
2. Then separate the eggs, & avoid mixing the yolk with the egg whites,

& then place the egg white inside a clean bowl.

3. With the aid of a clean non-greasy electric whisk, simply whisk the egg white with the tartar cream until the mix becomes stiff.

4. This step is important. Get a separate bowl and inside make use of the same whisk to mix together the cream cheese, yolk, salt, & until the mix is perfectly smooth.

5. Now with the aid of a spatula or spoon, gently fold the egg whites into the cream cheese mix, & make sure you work on batches- place a mound of egg whites at the top of the yolk mix, & then fold the yolk mix gently from underneath.

6. And on top of the egg white, while rotating the bowl, gain & again until the mixture has been perfectly incorporated.

7. Then make use of the folding technique in order to ensure that the

air bubbles remain intact inside the egg white.

8. Spoon 6 large mounds of the mix onto the already prepared baking sheet, & gently press the spoon or spatula on top of each of the mound to flatten it slightly.

9. One thing remains to be done now. Bake the bread rolls for between 30 & 40 minutes until they turn golden brown, then cool the rolls for some minutes on cooking sheet, & before transferring them unto wire rack.

10. Finally you may want to store leftovers inside a Ziploc bag in the fridge.

Servings: 6 to 8

Preparation time: 50 to 60 minutes

Simple yet tasty recipe.

Iconic Ultimate Ice Cream Fat Bomb

Wizard of all recipes.

Ingredients:

- 4 yolks from pastured eggs
- 8 to 10 ice cubes
- 1/3 cup coconut oil, melted
- 1/3 cup cacao butter, melted
- 1/3 cup of flavor mixture (combine cacao powder and your favorite tea leaves)
- About 1/2 cup MCT oil
- 15 to 20 drops of stevia
- 4 eggs, whole, pastured
- 2 teaspoons vanilla bean powder

Directions:

1. First of all, please make sure you have all the ingredients available. Use a blender to puree all the ingredients except the ice cubes. You should aim for a creamy mixture.

2. Now keep the blender running & start putting one ice cube at a time in it.
3. You want to make the mixture cold & moderately diluted.
4. This step is important. If you don't have space at the top of the lid, you should turn off the blender each time when you are adding an ice cube.
5. Then transfer the mixture into the ice cream maker & turn it on high for about 25 to 30 minutes.
6. Alternatively, you can put it in some kind of a loaf pan & keep it in the freezer.
7. Now however, in this case, you should freeze it for about 3.5 hours and stir every 30 to 35 minutes.
8. One thing remains to be done now. You can keep it in the freezer for up to a week.

9. Finally make sure always to serve it cold.

Serves: 3 to 5

Another fantastic recipe for you guys…

Awesome Cinnamon Bars

Magical taste.

Ingredients:

- 1/2 cup creamed coconut
- 2 tablespoons coconut oil, extra virgin
- About 1.5 tablespoon almond butter
- 2/3 teaspoon cinnamon

Directions:

1. First of all, please make sure you have all the ingredients available. Use muffin liners or something similar to line a mini loaf pan or a dish.
2. Then combine 1/8 teaspoon of cinnamon & creamed coconut in a bowl.
3. Transfer into the liners.
4. The amount is enough for 2 sections of the mini loaf pan.
5. This step is important. Use another bowl to combine almond

butter & 1 tablespoon of coconut oil.

6. Now spread it over the coconut mixture & place the pan into the freezer for about 10 to 15 minutes.

7. In the meantime, mix 1 tablespoon of coconut oil & 1/2 teaspoon of cinnamon in another bowl.

8. One thing remains to be done now. Then sprinkle over the bars & serve.

9. Finally alternatively, you can leave it in the freezer to further cool down.

Serves: 2 bars

Vintage overload…

Super Salted Coconut Almond Bark

What do you think?

Ingredients:

- 1/2 cup unsweetened coconut flakes
- About 1/2 teaspoon coarse sea salt
- 1/2 cup almonds
- About 1 teaspoon almond extract
- 2 cups (100 grams) 80-90% dark chocolate
- 10 drops liquid sweetener (optional and to taste)
- 1/2 cup coconut butter

Directions:

1. First of all, please make sure you have all the ingredients available. Start by setting the oven to about 340 to 350 degrees so it can preheat.

2. Then line a baking sheet with foil & then spread the coconut and almonds across it.

3. Place these in the oven to toast.

4. This should take 5 to 10 minutes & you should stir every 2 to 5 minutes to prevent burning. Then, set this pan to the side so everything can cool.

5. Now start warming the chocolate in a double boiler.

6. This step is important. Once most of it is melted, stir in the coconut butter & mix until smooth.

7. Add the sweetener if you choose & the almond extract.

8. Stir to incorporate thoroughly & set to the side while you prepare a pan.

9. Line a baking sheet with parchment paper & pour the dark chocolate mixture into it. Now please use a spatula to create an even layer.

10. Now evenly distribute the toasted coconut & almonds on top of the chocolate.
11. Finish this with a sprinkling of the sea salt.
12. One thing remains to be done now. Place this in the fridge for at least an hour.
13. Finally once it is set, you can slice it with a knife or break it into pieces.

Time for an iconic recipe.

Delightful Flavoured Coconut Fudge
Delicious recipe is ready.

Ingredients:

- 1 cup coconut oil
- About 1/2 cup Swerve confectioners
- 1/4 cup organic cocoa powder
- 1 tsp vanilla extract
- About 1 tsp almond extract
- 1/4 cup full at coconut milk
- 1/2 tsp Celtic sea salt

Directions:

1. First of all, please make sure you have all the ingredients available. Use a hand blender to mix the coconut oil & coconut milk till they form a glossy paste.
2. Then add the remaining ingredients in the bowl & stir on low speed till the cocoa is fully incorporated.
3. This step is important. Now please line a loaf pan with parchment paper & then spread the mixture in it.

4. Then place the pan in freezer for about 15 to 20 minutes, making sure that the fudge is properly set.
5. One thing remains to be done now. Remove from fridge & then cut the fudge into your desired sized pieces.
6. Finally you can also store the pieces in airtight container for long time.

Total time: 20 to 30 mins

Servings: 10 to 12

A style statement.

Nutrition per Serving:

Protein: 0.4g

Fat: 19.6g

Carbohydrate: 1.3g Net

Fantastic Tasty Peppermint Patties

Have you made it yet?

Ingredients:

- 4-oz 100% dark chocolate
- 1/2 c coconut butter
- About 2.5 tbsp raw honey
- 1/4 c shredded coconut, unsweetened
- 1 tsp peppermint extract
- About 2.5 tbsp coconut oil
- 4 tbsp coconut oil

Directions:

1. First of all, please make sure you have all the ingredients available. Soften two tablespoons of coconut oil and the coconut butter and mix in the honey, peppermint, & shredded coconut.
2. Now place two teaspoons of the mixture into the bottom of mini muffin cups & refrigerate for an hour.

3. This step is important. Make sure it's solid before you continue.
4. Then melt the dark chocolate & 4 tablespoons of coconut oil and combine well.
5. Place a teaspoon of the chocolate in the mini muffin cups.
6. One thing remains to be done now. Refrigerate for another hour.
7. Finally once solid, repeat the process until you're out of ingredients.

Servings: 22 to 24

Who wants to try this one?

Great Almond Butter & Cocoa Fat Bomb

The next big recipe…

Ingredients:

- 9 Tbsp. melted butter, salted
- 1 cup coconut oil (Melted)
- 3 Tbsp. cocoa powder
- About 1 tsp. liquid Stevia
- 200g almond butter

Directions:

1. First of all, please make sure you have all the ingredients available. Take a medium-sized pot & combine coconut oil together with the almond butter & cocoa powder
2. Then put the above-prepared mixture in a small sized blender of a food processor
3. Add melted butter & Stevia drops to the blender

4. This step is important. Process the mixture in the food processor until the mixture is smooth

5. Now pour down about 2.5 tablespoons of the mixture into the muffin molds (silicon candy mold recommended as they give the best results, paper muffin cups could be used too)

6. Place the molds in deep freezer & freeze them for around 40 to 45 minutes

7. Then pop out the fat bombs after deep freezing & store them in a container

8. One thing remains to be done now. Keep the container in refrigerator if you relish them frozen or keep them outside if you like them to melt soon while eating

9. Finally these fat bombs are about 90% fat, hence, shouldn't be consumed in large quantities

Total cooking & preparation time: 1 hour 15 to 20 minutes

Total servings: 24 to 26

Certainly a show stopper.

Nutrition facts (estimated amount per serving):

13.2g Total Fat

10.3g Saturated Fat

0.5g Protein

0g Trans Fat

0.2g Carbohydrates

14mg Cholesterol

0.1g Dietary Fiber

123 Calories

31mg Sodium

25mg Potassium

0.1g Sugars

Happy Zest And Zany Lemon Cheesecake Fat Bombs

I use to have it during my exams.

Ingredients:

- 4 tbsp melted unsalted butter
- About 2.5 tbsp Splenda or whatever sugar sub you use
- 4 oz softened cream cheese
- About 1.5 tbsp lemon juice
- Zest of about 1/2 a lemon
- 1/4 cup melted coconut oil

Directions:

1. First of all, please make sure you have all the ingredients available. Now combine all ingredients & mix with a hand mixer until nice and smooth.

2. One thing remains to be done now. Then portion into silicone tray
3. Finally freeze until firm

You can make this very easily.

Lucky Vanilla Nut Mixed Butter

Ready, set, go….

Ingredients:

- 8 to 10 Brazil Nuts
- About 1/2 Teaspoon Salt
- 1/2 Teaspoon Vanilla Extract
- 2 Cups Macadamia Nuts

Directions:

1. First of all, please make sure you have all the ingredients available. Now start by placing your macadamias, Brazil nuts, vanilla, and salt in a food processor, & start to blend.
2. Blend until you get your desired consistency.
3. One thing remains to be done now. Then it'll take about 2 to 5 minutes depending on how smooth you want it.

4. Finally you can store at room temperature for about a week, but you can always store it in the fridge for a month.

Prep Time: 5 to 10 Minutes

Total Time: 5 to 10 Minutes

Serves: 10 to 12

A little different, a little extra ordinary.

Nutritional Information:

Total Fat: 26 g

Protein: 8 g

Total Carbs: 3 g

Calories: 225

Vintage Butter Pecan Fat Bombs

A simple recipe which you will like.

Ingredients:

- Pinch of sea salt
- About 1.5 tbs unsalted butter (Softened)
- 1 tsp orange zest, finely grated
- 2 oz neufchâtel cheese
- 8 pecan halves

Directions:

1. First of all, please make sure you have all the ingredients available. Toast the pecans at 340 to 350 degrees Fahrenheit for about 5 to 10 minutes, check often to prevent burning.
2. Now mix the butter, neufchâtel cheese, & orange zest until smooth and creamy.

3. One thing remains to be done now. Then spread the butter mixture between the cooled pecan halves & sandwich together.
4. Finally sprinkle with sea salt & enjoy!

Servings: 2 to 4

A fine recipe, it just works.

Nutrition Facts (per serving)

Total Carbohydrates: 3,31g

Dietary Fiber: 1,5g

Net Carbs: 1,4g

Protein: 3g

Total Fat: 26g

Calories: 243

Best Low Carb Coconut Flour Flatbread

Yummy, definitely yummy.

Ingredients:

- 2 tablespoons of milk.
- About 1.5 teaspoon of coconut flour,
- 2 pinches of salt, and
- Optional 1 teaspoon of Parmesan cheese,
- 1/8 teaspoon of baking soda,
- Tablespoon of butter.
- About 1/4 teaspoon of baking powder,
- 1 medium to large egg,

Directions:

1. First of all, please make sure you have all the ingredients available. Add all the ingredients & stir them until there are no lumps, let the

batter sit for about a minute & you will notice it getting fluffier.

2. Now melt the butter, inside the pan before pouring 2 small size sandwich-size pancakes unto the pan.

3. This step is important. Now please place the pan on medium heat & when the top of it starts to bubble, simply flip the mix over.

4. Then put the cheese alongside the other contents on a slice, before putting the second flat bread on top.

5. One thing remains to be done now. Butter both flat bread pieces before you flip it.

6. Finally flip the sandwich flat bread when the bottom is turning brown & continue cooking until the cheese has completely melted.

Servings: 2 to 4

Preparation time: 1 to 2 hour

Don't wait, eat it!!

Nostalgic Almond Pistachio Fat Bombs

Just make it once and you will keep making it!!

Ingredients:

- 1/2 cup cocoa butter (Melted)
- 1/4 teaspoon salt
- 1 cup creamy coconut butter
- About 2.5 teaspoon chai spice
- 1/4 cup pistachios (Chopped)
- 1 cup coconut oil
- About 1/2 teaspoon almond extract
- 1/3 cup ghee
- 1/2 cup coconut milk, full-fat, chilled
- 1 tablespoon vanilla extract
- 1 cup almond butter, roasted

Directions:

1. First of all, please make sure you have all the ingredients available. Use parchment paper to line a baking pan (I recommend 9" square one).

61

2. Then make sure to leave a bit of paper hanging on each side to make unmolding easier.

3. Use a small saucepan to melt the cocoa butter over low heat.

4. This step is important. Alternatively, you can melt it in the microwave. Make sure to stir often.

5. Now use a big bowl to combine all ingredients except pistachios & cocoa butter.

6. Mix until well combined (use a hand mixer). Your aim is to make the mixture airy & light.

7. Then add the cocoa butter & continue mixing until it is well blended.

8. Equally distribute the mixture over the man.

9. Now drizzle chopped pistachios over the mixture.

10. One thing remains to be done now. Put it in the fridge & chill it

for at least 5.5 hours. You can also keep it overnight.

11. Finally cut the fat bombs into squares & serve.

Serves: 24 to 36 squares

I've always loved them. Plus they can be eaten anytime!!

Mighty Coconut Fat Bombs

Good luck!!

Ingredients:

- Salt to taste
- 1/4 cup butter
- About 1/2 teaspoon vanilla bean powder or cinnamon
- 1/4 cup coconut oil, extra virgin
- 1 1/2 cup flaked or shredded coconut, unsweetened

Directions:

1. First of all, please make sure you have all the ingredients available. Turn your oven to 340 to 350F. Line a baking sheet with parchment paper.
2. Now spread the coconut on the sheet & toast in in the oven for about 5 to 10 minutes.
3. You should go for a light golden color.

4. Make sure to stir a couple of times to avoid burning.
5. This step is important. Move the coconut into a blender & make it smooth.
6. Then add coconut oil & butter which you should cut into pieces.
7. Add vanilla or cinnamon & salt to your taste.
8. If you are feeling like having something sweet, you can also add a healthy sweetener, such as Stevia or Erythritol.
9. Now use molds to make a form of mini muffins from the mixture.
10. You can use a spoon, & you will get around 12 servings as long as you use 1 1/2 tablespoons for each fat bomb.
11. One thing remains to be done now. Keep it in the fridge for about 30 to 40 minutes.
12. Finally once it solidifies, serve the dish.

Serves: 10 to 12

Oh yeah!!

King Sized Raspberry Cheesecake Truffles

Stupidly simple...

Ingredients:

<u>For the filling:</u>

- 1 cup full-fat cream cheese (Softened)
- Liquid artificial sweetener to taste
- 1/2 cup almond flour
- About 1.5 teaspoon sugar-free vanilla extract
- 1/4 cup coconut flour
- 1 cup raspberries (Frozen)
- About 2.5 tablespoons powdered sugar substitute of your choice

<u>For the coating:</u>

- 2.8 ounces 90% dark chocolate
- 1.4 ounces cocoa butter

Directions:

1. First of all, please make sure you have all the ingredients available. Add the raspberries, sugar substitute, cream cheese, and vanilla to a food processor & process until smooth.
2. Now add the flours and pulse just long enough to mix them into the raspberry mixture.
3. Add 2 tablespoons of the mixture to an ice cube tray, cake pop molds, or other silicone molds.
4. Place these in the freezer for about 45 to 50 minutes to an hour to firm up before the next step.
5. This step is important. When you are almost ready to coat the truffles, warm the cocoa butter & dark chocolate in a double boiler.
6. Then once they melt completely, turn off the stove & let the mixture cool slightly.
7. You do not want it to solidify, but you also do not want it to be hot

enough to melt the raspberry truffles while you are coating them.

8. Now before you get started with the coating, line a baking tray with parchment paper & set it to the side.

9. Use a fork or toothpick to pierce the truffles in turn.

10. Then coat them one at a time, holding the raspberry ball over the bowl of chocolate & spooning the chocolate on top of it.

11. You will need to turn the ball to coat it completely.

12. Now you can stop turning once the chocolate solidifies.

13. One thing remains to be done now. Place the finished truffle on the prepared baking tray.

14. Finally once you are done, return the truffles to the refrigerator for at least 15 to 20 minutes to set before enjoying.

Be unique, be extraordinary…

Crazy Toasted Nutty Fudge

Something is special!!

Ingredients:

- 1/2 tsp Himalayan salt
- Few drops of almond extract
- 6 cups of toasted coconut flakes (unsweetened)
- About 1 tsp ground cinnamon
- 1/4 cup raw honey
- 1/2 cup ghee

Directions:

1. First of all, please make sure you have all the ingredients available. Grease a baking pan with coconut oil & then line it with parchment paper.
2. Then process the toasted coconut flakes in a food processor making sure that it become very smooth.
3. Add the cinnamon, salt, ghee & almond extract and process for a few more seconds.

70

4. This step is important. Add the honey & process for half minute.
5. Then you will notice drastic change in the consistency of the mixture.
6. It will actually become very thick & will even show signs of breaking up.
7. Now but this is what we need.
8. One thing remains to be done now. Spread the mixture on the prepared baking pan & allow setting overnight.
9. Finally on the next day, remove the fudge from the baking pan, discard the parchment paper & cut it into 36 equal sizes to serve.

Total time: 20 to 30 mins

Servings: 34

If you're a legend, then make this one.

Nutrition per Serving

Protein: 0.9g

Fat: 12.6g

Carbohydrate: 5.5g Net

Pinnacle Tasty Ketogenic Style Coconut Fat Bomb

Being lucky is definitely better.

Ingredients:

- 1 1/2 c shredded coconut, unsweetened
- About 1/2 tsp cinnamon
- 1/4 c butter
- 1/4 c extra virgin coconut oil
- Salt

Directions:

1. First of all, please make sure you have all the ingredients available. Your oven should be at 340 to 350.
2. Then spread the coconut on a baking sheet & bake it for about 5 to 10 minutes, or until it has browned slightly.
3. Stir it a couple of times so that it doesn't burn.

4. This step is important. Place the coconut in a food processor & mix until it is smooth and runny.
5. Now mix in the coconut oil and butter.
6. Stir in the salt, cinnamon, & some stevia if you want it a little bit sweeter.
7. One thing remains to be done now. Then pour the mixture into mini muffin forms & refrigerate for about 30 to 35 minutes.
8. Finally once done, remove from the forms & store in the refrigerator.

Servings: 10 to 12

Mystery is unveiled!!

Perfect Coconut Almond Keto Bomb

The speed matters…

Ingredients:

- 6 Tbsp. coconut butter
- 2 Tbsp. Sugar-free syrup
- About 1.5 Tbsp. cocoa powder
- 20 g chocolate, preferably dark
- 2 oz cream cheese
- About 6.5 Tbsp. almond butter

Directions:

1. First of all, please make sure you have all the ingredients available. Add cocoa powder, almond butter, cheese and dark chocolate in a medium sized pan
2. Now avoid adding coconut butter as we have to heat the mixture and fibers in the coconut tends to burn out
3. Add sugar-free syrup to the mixture & prepare a nice thick batter

4. This step is important. Take out the batter from the pan & put it in a microwavable dish

5. Then microwave the mixture in 10 to 15 seconds interval, taking out the mixture & stirring each time until the cheese and chocolate has sufficiently melted

6. At this point, add coconut butter to the mixture & stir it nicely (use a butter knife to ease the mixing and scraping process)

7. Now pour 2 tablespoons of the batter into the muffin trays (Above quantity mentioned of the ingredients will serve 12)

8. Place the tray in deep freeze & let it be there for about an hour

9. Then pop out the fat bombs from the tray & store in a container

10. One thing remains to be done now. Refrigerate the fat bomb candies after serving to make them last longer

11. Finally these are packed with nutrition from almond, coconut & dark chocolate and are worth eating in small quantities

Total cooking & preparation time: 1 hour & 30 to 40 minutes

Total servings: 12 to 14

Be super

Nutrition facts (estimated amount per serving):

11.2g Total Fat

5.3g Saturated Fat

81mg Potassium

2.8g Protein

0g Trans Fat

125 Calories

2.3g Dietary Fiber

6mg Cholesterol

24mg Sodium

4.3g Carbohydrates

1.2g Sugars

Thanks for reading my book.

Made in the USA
San Bernardino, CA
06 June 2018